Author's Note

This book contains 100 quotes by ex navy seal David Goggins. After reading this you will be undoubtedly more motivated and inspired to achieve your dreams

1

"The only way to achieve the impossible is to believe it is possible."

2

"Don't let your past dictate who you are, but let it be part of who you will become."

3

"When you think you're done, you're only at 40% of your total potential."

4

"The most important conversation is the one you have with yourself."

5

"We are either the masters of our suffering, or we are victims of it."

6

"If you can see yourself doing something, you can do it. If you can't see yourself doing it, usually you can't achieve it."

7

"We live in a world where mediocrity is often rewarded. Don't be afraid to be different."

8

"The only thing that's keeping you from getting what you want is the story you keep telling yourself."

9

"The mind is the most powerful weapon in the world. Once you've overcome the mental barriers, no obstacle is insurmountable."

10

"Do things that suck, because it's in the suck that growth happens."

11

"There's a whole new world on the other side of suffering."

12

"Life is a battle between trying to find more of yourself and trying to lose yourself. Let's make sure we're losing the right things."

13

"It's okay to be driven by fear, but you have to be driven by a bigger purpose."

14

"The only person you are destined to become is the person you decide to be."

15

"You are in danger of living a life so comfortable and soft, that you will die without ever realizing your true potential."

16

"Stop feeling sorry for yourself and you will be happy."

17

"The worst thing you can do is make excuses for anything. No excuses. No explanation."

18

"Greatness pulls mediocrity into the mud. Get out there and get after it."

19

"Life is about finding your own path, not following someone else's."

20

"You have to prove yourself every single day, through your actions."

21

"Your mind is your best weapon. Your thoughts can either be your most powerful asset or your greatest weakness."

22

"We have to realize that we are responsible for the life we have created."

23

"Don't count the days. Make the days count."

24

"Comfort zones are deadly. If you allow your brain to get too comfortable, your brain will find a way to sabotage you."

25

"If you're looking for a way out, you're already dead."

26

"Be willing to go all out, in pursuit of your dream. Ultimately, it will pay off. You are more powerful than you think."

27

"The only limitations that you have are the ones you put on yourself."

28

"Don't run from challenges, run toward them. The only way to escape fear is to trample it beneath your feet."

29

"Obsession is a term the lazy use to describe the dedicated."

30

"It's not about perfect. It's about effort. And when you bring that effort every single day, that's where transformation happens. That's how change occurs."

31

"If you're not where you want to be in life, double down on what got you there."

32

"There is no more time to waste. Hours and days evaporate like creeks in the desert. That's why it's okay to be obsessed about your dream."

33

"In order to be who you are capable of becoming, you must first understand who you are."

34

"You have to be willing to fail, to be hurt, to crash and burn, to have people laugh at you -- that's part of the process."

35

"There's so much more out there than failing."

36

"It's not about the cards you're dealt, but how you play the hand."

37

"The cookie jar is always there. You've got to be able to tell yourself, 'No.'"

38

"I'm not great. I don't do anything great. I'm not the strongest. I'm not the fastest. I'm just willing to suffer in order to achieve my goals."

39

"Suffering is a test. That's all it is. Suffering is the true test of life."

40

"Most of this generation quits the second they get talked to. It's so easy to be great nowadays because most people are just weak, and if you have any mental toughness, if you have any fraction of self-discipline; the ability to not want to do it, but still do it, you're gonna be successful."

41

"When you think you're done, you're only at 40% of your body's capability."

42

"Life is not a race. Neither is it a marathon nor a sprint. Life is a relentless, forward moving action and it's up to you to match that action with your own."

43

"The only way you're gonna get to the other side of this journey is by suffering."

44

"The most important thing you can do in your life is learn how to endure pain."

45

"Being afraid of the unknown is a luxury."

46

"We have a lack of mental toughness in the world right now."

47

"The reason why I talk about myself so much is because I lived in the darkest hell. That's what I want people to resonate with."

48

"You will never learn from people if you always tap dance around the truth."

49

"I'm not afraid of failing.
I'm not afraid of anything in
this world."

50

"You have to make sure your worst enemy doesn't live between your own two ears."

51

"Stop giving yourself the easy way out."

52

"Motivation is crap.
Motivation comes and goes.
When you're driven,
whatever is in front of you
will get destroyed."

53

"One of the things I realized early on is that I was willing to outwork anybody, even if it meant going to a level that I couldn't physically reach, and then figuring out a way to get there."

54

"The purpose of accountability is not to make you feel like shit, it's to make you grow."

55

"Life is a big tug of war between mediocrity and trying to find your greatness."

56

"I realized that I was the problem. The way that I was approaching things, the way I was going about things, my mindset, it was all about getting by. I was getting by, and I realized that getting by sucks."

57

"The more you dream, the more you will achieve."

58

"I believe that there is a greater power constantly ready to test you to see if you can take the hit. You're gonna fail and fail and fail and fail, and you've got to be ready to take that hit."

59

"No one is going to believe in you more than you."

60

"There is a badge of honor in suffering."

61

"I'm all about getting out of your comfort zone."

62

"The things that we run from, we run into."

63

"You want to be uncommon amongst uncommon people."

64

"You have to be willing to suffer long-term pain for long-term gain."

65

"You are your only opponent. Stop competing against others, and start competing against yourself."

66

"We have one life. You gotta live it to the fullest. You gotta squeeze every ounce of life out of it."

67

"The people who are grinding, day in and day out, are the ones who are more successful. They're the ones who will never quit."

68

"Everyone's trying to get to the top of the mountain, but there's so much respect for the grind of climbing that mountain."

69

"Every morning in our lives, we have a choice to make. You have the choice to stay in bed and say, 'Forget it, I'm not going to work out today.' Or 'Forget it, I'm not going to work hard today.' That's your choice that you make every single day of your life."

70

"You can't hurt me. I promise you."

71

"You have to find your own mental edge."

72

"We can be accountable for our actions only when we have the courage to confront our demons."

73

"Sometimes, life will beat you into submission. You don't need to beat yourself as well."

74

"The path to success will leave you callused, bruised, and very tired. But at the end of the day, when you look in the mirror, you will like the person staring back at you."

75

"You have to put yourself in an environment where you are the weak link."

76

"Fear is your ultimate guide in life."

77

"When you're great at something, you're going to tell the world about it. When you're great at something, they're going to tell you about it."

78

"Life is a battle between trying to find more of yourself and trying to lose yourself."

79

"You don't realize it's a war going on. We all want to feel good, but in order to feel good, you have to get rid of the bullsh*t. It's a constant war. You're trying to fight against the worst parts of you to become the best part of you."

80

"Don't wait for things to get easier. You get better."

81

"Stop blaming everybody. Stop complaining and pointing the finger at somebody else. Become your own hero."

82

"I was a product of my own environment, and I chose that environment to train in."

83

"If you give anything less than your best, you're sacrificing the gift."

84

"Every morning, I wake up in my bed and I'm grateful for the day, but I also know it might be my last. I can't sleep past 4:30 or 5 a.m. because I feel like I'm wasting time."

85

"We're all great. No matter if you think you're dumb, if you think you're overweight, if you think you're not athletic – we're all great. And when you realize that you're great, you can do anything."

86

"Being uncommon starts with your mindset."

87

"If you're willing to go through all the battling you got to go through to get where you want to get, who's got the right to stop you?"

88

"We can all suffer, but the question is: can you recover from that suffering?"

89

"Your mission doesn't have to be saving the world or changing the world. It can be saving your own world and changing your own life."

90

"You can't make excuses and be great at the same time."

91

"You have to become the best version of yourself for you, and if you want to share that with people, that's cool."

92

"Every day of my life is a small life, and I make it that way."

93

"Life isn't about being soft. Life isn't about crying and giving up. Life is about finding a way through all the stuff you've been through and fighting."

94

"Don't be afraid to fail. Be afraid of not taking that shot."

95

"Your mind and your body are capable of anything."

96

"When you're tired, you don't want to train, that's when the real training starts."

97

"Life is not always fair, but it's always good when you're making decisions based on the journey you're on versus the moment you're in."

98

"You have to work to develop a mental edge."

99

"It's okay to be selfish with your time. It's okay to be ruthless with your goals. It's okay to be focused on your dreams and what you want."

100

"No one is coming to save you. Only you can save you."

Manufactured by Amazon.ca
Acheson, AB